THE GREEN RUSH

How to Make Money in the Legal Cannabis Business

LARRY REDDICK

AuthorHouse™
1663 Liberty Drive
Bloomington, IN 47403
www.authorhouse.com
Phone: 833-262-8899

Because of the dynamic nature of the Internet, any web addresses or links contained in this book may have changed since publication and may no longer be valid. The views expressed in this work are solely those of the author and do not necessarily reflect the views of the publisher, and the publisher hereby disclaims any responsibility for them.

Any people depicted in stock imagery provided by Getty Images are models, and such images are being used for illustrative purposes only.
Certain stock imagery © Getty Images.

This book is printed on acid-free paper.

ISBN: 979-8-8230-0397-1 (sc)
ISBN: 979-8-8230-0396-4 (e)

Library of Congress Control Number: 2023905013

Print information available on the last page.

Published by AuthorHouse 03/15/2023

authorHOUSE®

The Green Rush

How to Make Money in the Legal Cannabis Business

Larry Reddick

https://www.youtube.com/@lalivetime1

Table of Contents

Introduction

The legalization of cannabis in many parts of the world has led to a rapidly growing industry. With the cannabis market projected to reach $73.6 billion by 2027, there has never been a better time to enter the legal cannabis business. This book is a comprehensive guide on how to make money in the cannabis industry while staying within the bounds of the law.

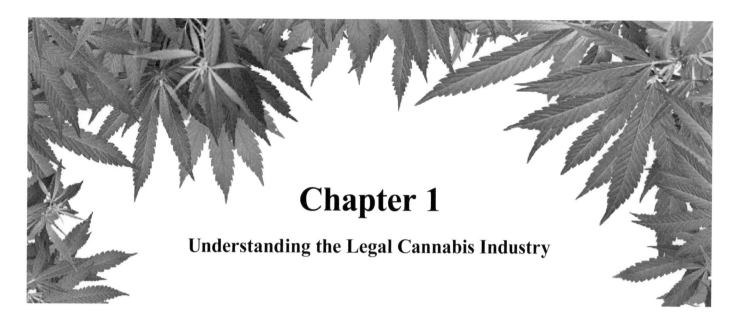

Chapter 1

Understanding the Legal Cannabis Industry

In this chapter, we will discuss the legal framework of the cannabis industry. We will explore the laws and regulations that govern the cultivation, distribution, and sale of cannabis. It is crucial to have a clear understanding of these regulations before entering the cannabis business.

Legal framework for the cannabis industry

The legal framework for the cannabis industry varies by country and state.

In some places, cannabis is completely illegal and any activities related to it are considered criminal offenses. In other places, cannabis is legal for medical use, but not for recreational use. And in some places, cannabis is legal for both medical and recreational use.

Here are some examples of the legal frameworks for the cannabis industry in different countries:

1. **Canada:** Cannabis is legal for both medical and recreational use. The Cannabis Act regulates the production, distribution, and sale of cannabis in Canada.

2. **United States:** Cannabis is illegal at the federal level, but many states have legalized it for medical and/or recreational use. Each state has its own regulations for the cannabis industry.

3. **Uruguay:** Cannabis is legal for both medical and recreational use. The government regulates the production, distribution, and sale of cannabis.

4. **Netherlands:** Cannabis is technically illegal, but the government has a policy of tolerance for small amounts of cannabis for personal use. Coffee shops are allowed to sell cannabis, but the production and distribution of cannabis is still illegal.

5. **Israel:** Cannabis is legal for medical use. The government regulates the production and distribution of medical cannabis.

These are just a few examples, and the legal framework for the cannabis industry is constantly changing and evolving in many places. It's important to check the laws and regulations in your specific location before engaging in any activities related to cannabis.

Laws and regulations for the cannabis business

Laws and regulations regarding the cannabis business vary by country and jurisdiction. In many places, cannabis remains illegal for both medical and recreational use. However, there are some areas where cannabis has been legalized or decriminalized, and regulations have been put in place to govern its production, sale, and consumption. Here are some examples:

United States:

In the United States, cannabis is illegal at the federal level but legal for medical or recreational use in some states. Each state has its own laws and regulations regarding the cannabis industry. For example, some states require cannabis businesses to obtain licenses, follow specific safety and security protocols, and pay taxes on their sales.

Canada:

In Canada, cannabis was legalized for recreational use in 2018. The federal government sets minimum standards for the production, sale, and distribution of cannabis, but each province and territory can also establish its own rules and regulations.

European Union:

In the European Union, cannabis laws vary by country. Some countries have legalized medical cannabis, while others have decriminalized possession of small amounts of cannabis. The EU does not have a unified approach to regulating cannabis, but it has issued guidelines for member states to follow.

Australia:

In Australia, cannabis laws vary by state and territory. Some states have legalized medical cannabis, while others have decriminalized possession of small amounts of cannabis. The federal government regulates the production, import, and export of cannabis for medical purposes.

Overall, the cannabis industry is heavily regulated in most places where it is legal. Businesses must comply with a range of rules and regulations to ensure the safety and quality of their products and to avoid legal issues.

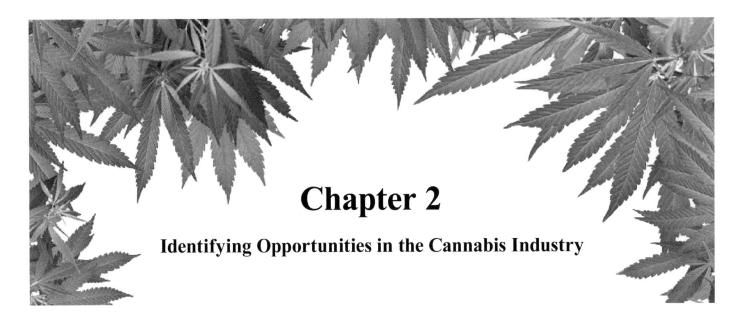

Chapter 2

Identifying Opportunities in the Cannabis Industry

In this chapter, we will identify the different opportunities available in the cannabis industry. From cultivation and processing to distribution and retail, we will explore the various sectors of the industry and the potential for profitability in each.

Cultivation of the cannabis industry

The cultivation of the cannabis industry involves the growing and harvesting of cannabis plants for various purposes, including medical, recreational, and industrial use. The industry has grown significantly in recent years due to the increasing legalization of cannabis in various countries and states.

There are various methods of cultivation in the cannabis industry, including indoor, outdoor, and greenhouse growing. Indoor cultivation involves growing cannabis plants in a controlled environment, typically using artificial lighting and climate control systems. Outdoor cultivation involves growing cannabis plants outside in natural sunlight, while greenhouse cultivation involves growing cannabis plants in a controlled environment using natural sunlight.

Cannabis cultivation requires knowledge of plant genetics, soil chemistry, pest control, and cultivation techniques. Growers must also adhere to regulations related to pesticide use, water usage, and waste disposal.

The cannabis industry includes various segments, including cultivators, processors, distributors, and retailers. Many companies in the industry are vertically integrated, meaning they handle multiple segments of the supply chain. As the cannabis industry continues to grow, it is expected to create new jobs, generate tax revenue, and provide new opportunities for businesses and investors. However, the industry also faces challenges related to regulatory compliance, banking access, and market volatility.

Processing cannabis legally

The legality of processing cannabis depends on the laws of the specific jurisdiction in which you are located. In some areas, processing cannabis is legal for medical or recreational use, while in others it is strictly prohibited.

If cannabis processing is legal in your area, there are likely regulations and requirements that must be followed in order to operate a legal cannabis processing business. These requirements may include obtaining a license or permit, complying with safety and sanitation standards, and following specific processing and labeling guidelines.

It is important to consult with a lawyer or regulatory agency in your area to ensure that you are operating legally and in compliance with all applicable laws and regulations. Additionally, it is important to note that cannabis laws are subject to change, so it is important to stay up to date on any changes or developments in your area's regulations.

Legal distribution of cannabis

The legal distribution of cannabis, including its production, sale, possession, and use, varies by country and jurisdiction.

In some countries, such as Canada and Uruguay, cannabis has been fully legalized for recreational use, meaning that individuals can purchase and consume cannabis products without fear of prosecution. Other countries, such as the Netherlands and Portugal, have decriminalized cannabis possession and use, meaning that individuals may possess and use small amounts of cannabis without fear of criminal charges, but distribution and sale remain illegal.

In the United States, cannabis is still illegal at the federal level, but many states have legalized it for either medical or recreational use. In states where cannabis is legal, it can be sold through licensed dispensaries, which are regulated by the state government. However, transporting cannabis across state lines is still illegal, even if the drug is legal in both states.

It is important to note that even in jurisdictions where cannabis is legal, there may be restrictions on its use, such as age limits, limits on the amount that can be possessed or purchased, and restrictions on where it can be consumed. Additionally, driving under the influence of cannabis is illegal in all jurisdictions, regardless of its legal status.

Retail in the cannabis industry

The cannabis industry has seen significant growth in recent years, particularly with the legalization of cannabis in many parts of the world. As a result, the retail sector has emerged as an important component of the industry. Here are some key aspects of retail in the cannabis industry:

1. **Dispensaries:** Dispensaries are the primary retail outlets for **cannabis products.** These stores vary widely in terms of size, design, and product offerings. Some dispensaries specialize in medical cannabis products, while others cater to recreational users. Dispensaries must comply with strict regulations and laws regarding the sale and distribution of cannabis products.

2. **Online sales:** Online sales have become increasingly popular in the cannabis industry, particularly in areas where dispensaries are limited or not allowed. Online retailers typically offer a wide range of products, including cannabis flower, edibles, concentrates, and more. These retailers must also comply with strict regulations regarding age verification and shipping.

3. **Branding and marketing:** As the cannabis industry becomes more competitive, branding and marketing have become increasingly important for retailers. Retailers must create compelling brands and marketing campaigns to attract customers and differentiate themselves from competitors.

4. **Product variety:** The cannabis industry offers a wide variety of products, including flower, edibles, concentrates, and more. Retailers must offer a diverse range of products to meet the needs and preferences of their customers.

5. **Compliance and regulations:** Retailers must comply with strict regulations and laws regarding the sale and distribution of cannabis products. These regulations vary depending on the location and jurisdiction.

Overall, retail in the cannabis industry is a rapidly evolving sector that requires careful attention to compliance, branding, and marketing. As the industry continues to grow and mature, retailers will play an increasingly important role in shaping its future.

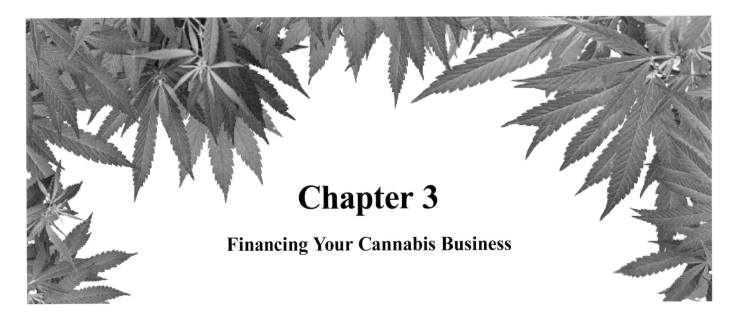

Chapter 3

Financing Your Cannabis Business

One of the biggest challenges in starting a cannabis business is financing. In this chapter, we will explore the different ways to finance a cannabis business. We will also discuss the financial risks associated with the cannabis industry and how to manage them.

Different ways to finance a cannabis business

The legality of cannabis varies across different jurisdictions, so the methods of financing a cannabis business may also vary. However, here are some possible ways to finance a cannabis business:

1. **Personal savings:** Starting a cannabis business can be expensive, so using personal savings may be a viable option for some entrepreneurs.

2. **Friends and family**: Some entrepreneurs may seek financial support from friends and family members who are willing to invest in their business.

3. **Angel investors**: Angel investors are individuals who invest in early-stage businesses in exchange for equity or ownership in the company. Some angel investors may be interested in investing in a cannabis business.

4. **Venture capital:** Venture capital firms are companies that invest in businesses with high growth potential. Some venture capital firms may be interested in investing in the cannabis industry.

5. **Private equity:** Private equity firms are companies that invest in established businesses with the goal of improving their operations and profitability. Some private equity firms may be interested in investing in the cannabis industry.

6. **Crowdfunding:** Crowdfunding is a method of raising money from a large number of people, typically through online platforms. Some crowdfunding platforms may allow cannabis businesses to raise funds.

Small Business Administration (SBA) loans: The SBA offers loans to small businesses, including those in the cannabis industry, through their 7(a) loan program. However, it's important to note that the legality of cannabis at the federal level may limit access to these loans.

- **Cannabis-specific lenders:** Some lenders specialize in providing loans and financing to cannabis businesses. These lenders may have a better understanding of the unique challenges and opportunities of the cannabis industry.

It's important to note that the legality of cannabis varies by jurisdiction, so entrepreneurs should consult with legal and financial experts to determine the best financing options for their specific situation.

Financial risks associated with the cannabis industry

The cannabis industry is a rapidly growing sector with immense potential for investors. However, like any emerging industry, it also carries a range of financial risks that investors should be aware of. Here are some of the most significant financial risks associated with the cannabis industry:

1. **Legal and Regulatory Risks:** One of the most significant risks facing the cannabis industry is the uncertainty surrounding the legality of cannabis at the federal level in the United States. While many states have legalized cannabis for medical or recreational use, it is still illegal under federal law. As a result, cannabis companies may face legal and regulatory challenges that could affect their operations, profitability, and market share.

2. **Market Risks:** The cannabis industry is subject to the same market risks as any other industry. These include changes in consumer demand, competitive pressures, and economic conditions that could impact the industry's growth and profitability.

3. **Operational Risks:** Cannabis companies face operational risks associated with the cultivation, production, and distribution of cannabis. These risks include pests and diseases, natural disasters, and supply chain disruptions that could impact production and revenue.

4. **Financial Risks:** Cannabis companies face financial risks associated with funding their operations, including the difficulty of obtaining financing from traditional lenders and the high cost of capital associated with the industry.

5. **Reputation Risks:** The cannabis industry is subject to reputation risks, including negative perceptions of the industry, as well as potential adverse effects of cannabis use on individuals and society.

Overall, investors should be aware of the risks associated with the cannabis industry and conduct thorough due diligence before investing.

Chapter 4

Choosing the Right Business Model

In this chapter, we will explore the different business models available in the cannabis industry. From starting a dispensary to becoming a cannabis supplier, we will discuss the pros and cons of each business model and help you choose the right one for your goals.

Starting a Dispensary: Pros and Cons

Starting a dispensary can be a complex process, but here are some general steps to get you started:

1. **Research the laws and regulations in your state:** Before you start a dispensary, you need to ensure that it is legal to do so in your state. Research the laws and regulations related to the sale and distribution of cannabis in your area.

2. **Create a business plan:** A business plan is an essential tool for any business, and it will help you define your goals, target market, financial projections, and strategies for success.

3. **Secure funding:** Starting a dispensary can be expensive, so you'll need to secure funding from investors, loans, or personal funds. Ensure that you have enough capital to cover startup costs, such as rent, utilities, equipment, and inventory.

4. **Choose a location:** Select a location that is compliant with state regulations and zoning laws. Consider the local competition, accessibility, and safety of the area.

5. **Obtain necessary licenses and permits**: You'll need to apply for a license from the state's regulatory agency and any local permits required to operate your dispensary.

6. **Build your team:** Hire employees with experience in the cannabis industry, such as budtenders, managers, and security personnel.

Pros of starting a dispensary:

1. **Lucrative market:** The cannabis industry is growing rapidly, and the demand for cannabis products is increasing.

2. **Job creation:** Starting a dispensary can create jobs in your community.

3. **Social impact:** Cannabis can be used for medical and recreational purposes, and owning a dispensary can positively impact people's lives.

Cons of starting a dispensary:

1. **Legal challenges:** The cannabis industry is still subject to legal challenges and risks, and navigating the complex regulatory landscape can be challenging.

2. **High startup costs:** Starting a dispensary can be expensive, and funding can be difficult to secure.

3. **Limited access to banking:** Many financial institutions are hesitant to work with cannabis-related businesses, making it challenging to secure loans or banking services.

4. **Stigma:** Despite the growing acceptance of cannabis, there is still a social stigma attached to the industry, which can affect public perception and marketing efforts.

Becoming a cannabis supplier

Becoming a cannabis supplier involves several steps, and the specific requirements may vary depending on your location and the laws and regulations in your area.

Here are some general steps to consider:

1. **Research your local laws and regulations:** It's important to research the laws and regulations governing the production and distribution of cannabis in your area. This can include obtaining a license or permit and adhering to strict regulations around cultivation, packaging, and distribution.

2. **Develop a business plan:** Like any business, becoming a cannabis supplier requires careful planning. Consider your target market, product offerings, pricing strategy, and marketing plan. You'll also need to identify your funding sources and determine your budget for startup costs.

3. **Obtain necessary permits and licenses:** Depending on where you live, you may need to obtain a license or permit to produce or distribute cannabis. These requirements can vary widely, so it's important to research the specific regulations in your area.

4. **Secure a facility and equipment:** Once you've obtained the necessary permits, you'll need to find a suitable facility to grow and process your cannabis. This will require a significant investment in equipment, including lighting, irrigation systems, and ventilation.

5. **Cultivate and process your product:** With your facility and equipment in place, it's time to start growing and processing your cannabis. This can be a timeconsuming process, as cannabis requires careful attention to detail to ensure quality and potency.

Pros and cons of becoming a cannabis supplier:

Pros

- The cannabis industry is rapidly growing, providing opportunities for entrepreneurs to enter a new and potentially lucrative market.

- As a cannabis supplier, you have the opportunity to work in a unique and exciting field that is constantly evolving.

- Depending on the location, cannabis suppliers may face less competition than in other industries.

Cons

- The legal landscape surrounding cannabis can be complex and ever-changing, with significant regulatory hurdles to navigate.

- Cannabis suppliers may face social stigma or pushback from certain segments of the population.

- Depending on the location, cannabis suppliers may face significant competition from other businesses.

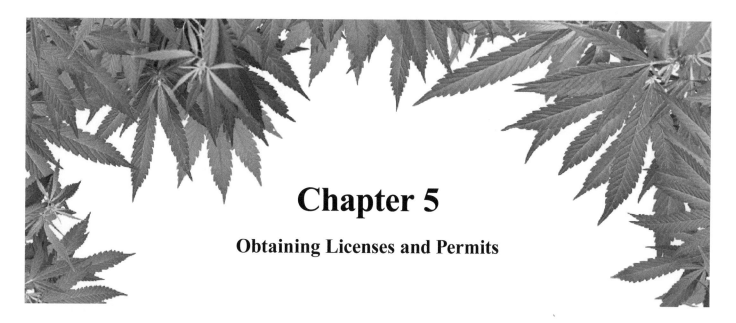

Chapter 5

Obtaining Licenses and Permits

The cannabis industry is highly regulated, and obtaining the necessary licenses and permits is a complex process. In this chapter, we will guide you through the process of obtaining the licenses and permits required to operate a legal cannabis business.

Cannabis Business Licensing and permits

The process of obtaining a license or permit for a cannabis business can vary depending on the country or state where you plan to operate. However, here are some general steps you can expect to follow:

1. **Research the laws and regulations:** Before you start the licensing process, it is important to understand the laws and regulations related to cannabis in your area. Make sure you understand the restrictions, requirements, and licensing fees involved.

2. **Determine the type of license you need:** There are typically different types of licenses for different aspects of the cannabis business, such as cultivation, manufacturing, distribution, and retail. Determine which type of license you need based on the type of business you plan to operate.

3. **Prepare your application:** Once you have determined the type of license you need, you will need to prepare your application. This may involve submitting information such as your business plan, financial statements, security plans, and background checks for all key personnel.

4. **Submit your application:** Once your application is complete, you will need to submit it to the appropriate regulatory agency. This may involve submitting it online, in person, or through the mail.

5. **Wait for approval:** Depending on the area you are in, the approval process can take weeks or months. During this time, the regulatory agency will review your application and may request additional information or clarification.

6. **Complete any additional requirements:** Once you receive approval, you may need to complete additional requirements before you can start operating your business. This may include inspections, training, or additional documentation.

7. **Obtain your license:** Once you have completed all requirements, you will receive your license or permit. Make sure to display it prominently in your business and follow all rules and regulations related to your license.

Overall, obtaining a license or permit for a cannabis business can be a complex and time-consuming process, but it is necessary to operate legally and responsibly in this industry.

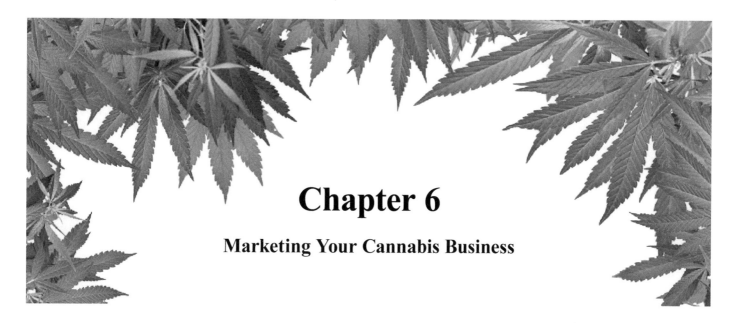

Chapter 6

Marketing Your Cannabis Business

Marketing is essential in any business, and the cannabis industry is no exception. In this chapter, we will explore the different marketing strategies for a cannabis business. We will discuss how to build a strong brand, advertise your products, and connect with customers.

Building a Cannabis Brand

Building a strong brand in the cannabis business requires careful planning and execution. Here are some steps you can take to establish a strong brand:

1. **Define your brand identity:** Your brand identity is the core of your brand. It includes your mission, vision, values, and personality. You need to define what sets your brand apart from others in the market, and how you want your customers to perceive your brand.

2. **Develop a unique visual identity:** Your visual identity includes your logo, colors, packaging, and overall design. Your visual identity should be unique, recognizable, and consistent across all your products and marketing materials.

3. **Build a strong online presence:** In the cannabis industry, many consumers do their research online before making a purchase. You need to have a strong online presence, including a website, social media accounts, and online listings.

4. **Offer quality products:** Your brand's reputation depends on the quality of your products. You need to ensure that your products are of high quality and meet the needs and expectations of your customers.

5. **Establish relationships with customers:** Building relationships with your customers is key to building a strong brand. You should engage with your customers through social media, email marketing, and other channels to build trust and loyalty.

6. **Develop a marketing strategy:** A marketing strategy is essential for promoting your brand and products. You should identify your target audience and develop campaigns that speak to their needs and interests.

7. **Stay compliant:** The cannabis industry is heavily regulated, and compliance is essential to building a strong brand. You need to ensure that your products and marketing materials comply with all relevant laws and regulations.

By following these steps, you can build a strong brand in the cannabis business that resonates with your target audience and sets you apart from your competitors.

Cannabis Advertising Guidelines

The advertising and marketing of cannabis products can be challenging due to the legal restrictions and regulations in different countries and states. In many places, cannabis is still illegal or only legal for medicinal purposes, so advertising cannabis products can be restricted.

Here are some tips to consider when advertising cannabis products:

1. **Know the laws:** It is important to understand the laws and regulations regarding the advertising of cannabis products in your state or country. Different regions may have different rules on what is allowed and what is not.

2. **Be mindful of your audience:** Make sure you target your advertising to an appropriate audience. Advertising to minors or promoting excessive use of cannabis can lead to legal issues.

3. **Use appropriate language and imagery:** Use language and imagery that is appropriate and in line with the brand image you want to portray. Avoid using language that suggests that cannabis is a cure for any health condition or that it is completely harmless.

4. **Be honest about the product:** Provide accurate and truthful information about the product, including any risks or side effects. Making false or misleading claims can damage your reputation and lead to legal problems.

5. **Consider alternative advertising methods:** Depending on the laws in your region, you may need to get creative with advertising. For example, some companies use social media or events to promote their products.

Overall, advertising in the cannabis industry can be challenging due to legal restrictions and social stigma, but it is possible to promote products in a responsible and effective way.

Connecting with Cannabis Customers

Connecting with customers in the cannabis business requires a thoughtful and strategic approach, given the unique regulatory and social landscape of the industry. Here are some tips to consider:

1. **Know your target audience:** Understanding who your customers are is key to connecting with them. Consider their age, gender, interests, and lifestyle to tailor your messaging and product offerings accordingly.

2. **Create engaging content:** In the digital age, content is king. Whether it's educational resources, social media posts, or product reviews, make sure your content is informative, entertaining, and shareable. This will help establish your brand as a trusted source of information and build a loyal customer base.

3. **Leverage social media:** Social media platforms like Instagram, Twitter, and Facebook can be powerful tools for reaching and engaging with customers. However, because of the strict

advertising guidelines in the cannabis industry, it's important to tread carefully and follow platform policies to avoid getting banned. Focus on creating high-quality content that resonates with your audience.

4. **Host events and workshops:** Hosting events and workshops is a great way to connect with customers inperson and provide them with hands-on experiences with your products. Consider partnering with other cannabis businesses and industry experts to create unique and informative events.

5. **Prioritize customer service:** Providing excellent customer service is crucial for building customer loyalty and retention. Make sure to respond promptly to customer inquiries, provide personalized recommendations, and always strive to exceed their expectations.

By taking a customer-centric approach and utilizing the right tools and strategies, you can successfully connect with your target audience and build a thriving cannabis business.

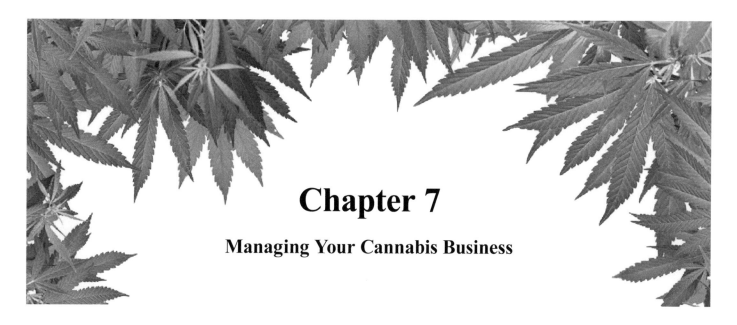

Chapter 7

Managing Your Cannabis Business

Running a successful cannabis business requires effective management. In this chapter, we will explore the different aspects of managing a cannabis business. From hiring and training employees to managing finances and inventory, we will provide you with the tools to run a successful business.

Hiring for Cannabis Business

Hiring and training employees for a cannabis business can be a unique process given the specific regulations and requirements that come with working in the cannabis industry. Here are some general tips to consider:

1. **Know the regulations:** Before hiring employees, make sure you are aware of the specific regulations in your state and municipality regarding cannabis businesses. This includes requirements for background checks, security clearances, and employee training.

2. **Hire for diversity:** As with any business, hiring a diverse workforce can help bring different perspectives and experiences to your team. Additionally, in the cannabis industry, having a diverse workforce can help overcome any negative stigma associated with cannabis use.

3. **Emphasize customer service:** Customer service is key in any industry, but it's especially important in the cannabis industry. Many customers may be new to cannabis and may have a lot of questions. Make sure your employees are trained to provide accurate and helpful information to customers.

4. **Provide training:** In addition to training employees on customer service, make sure they are properly trained on cannabis products, regulations, and safety procedures. This includes training on how to handle cash, inventory management, and security procedures.

5. **Create a positive company culture:** Cannabis businesses are often stigmatized, so creating a positive company culture is important for attracting and retaining employees. This can include offering competitive salaries and benefits, providing opportunities for growth and advancement, and fostering a supportive and inclusive work environment.

6. **Consider experience:** While experience in the cannabis industry can be helpful, it's not always necessary. Consider candidates with transferable skills such as experience in retail, hospitality, or healthcare.

7. **Build a strong team:** Building a strong team is essential for the success of any business. Look for candidates who are passionate about the industry, have a positive attitude, and are willing to learn and grow with the company.

Managing Finances in Cannabis

Managing finances in the cannabis business requires some unique considerations due to the industry's regulatory and legal landscape. Here are some tips on how to effectively manage your finances in the cannabis industry:

1. **Keep Accurate Records:** One of the most important things you can do is to keep detailed and accurate records of all your financial transactions. This includes income, expenses, and taxes. It is essential to track your finances carefully to ensure you are compliant with all local and federal regulations.

2. **Hire a Qualified Accountant:** It is important to work with a qualified accountant who is familiar with the cannabis industry's unique financial considerations. An experienced accountant can help you navigate complex tax laws, keep your books in order, and provide you with valuable financial advice.

3. **Manage Cash Flow:** Since cannabis is still illegal under federal law, most banks and financial institutions are hesitant to do business with cannabis companies. As a result, most cannabis businesses operate on a cashonly basis. It is important to manage your cash flow carefully and keep large sums of cash secure.

4. **Plan for the Future:** As the cannabis industry continues to evolve, it is important to plan for the future. This includes forecasting your future cash flow, managing your debt, and preparing for potential regulatory changes.

5. **Invest in Technology:** As with any business, investing in technology can help streamline your operations and increase efficiency. In the cannabis industry, technology can be particularly helpful in tracking inventory, managing compliance, and analyzing data.

By following these tips, you can effectively manage your finances in the cannabis industry and ensure the long-term success of your business.

Cannabis inventory management.

Managing inventory for a cannabis business involves careful planning and tracking to ensure that you have enough product on hand to meet demand while minimizing waste and avoiding overstocking. Here are some steps you can take to manage your inventory effectively:

1. **Set up a system for tracking inventory:** You can use a spreadsheet or specialized inventory software to track your cannabis products, including the strain, batch number, quantity, and expiration date.

2. **Conduct regular inventory audits:** Regularly auditing your inventory allows you to identify discrepancies and adjust your stock levels accordingly. It also helps you identify products that are not selling well or are nearing their expiration date.

3. **Implement a first-in, first-out (FIFO) system:** This means that the oldest products are sold first to ensure that they do not expire before they are sold.

4. **Forecast demand and adjust inventory levels accordingly:** Using sales data and historical trends, you can estimate how much product you will need for a given period and adjust your inventory levels accordingly.

5. **Develop relationships with suppliers:** Building relationships with suppliers allows you to negotiate better prices and ensures that you have a reliable source of inventory.

6. **Consider using automated inventory management systems:** Using automated systems can streamline the inventory management process and provide real-time data on your inventory levels, which can help you make better decisions about ordering and stocking.

7. **Stay compliant with state and local regulations:** Make sure you are aware of any regulations related to inventory tracking and reporting in your jurisdiction, and ensure that your inventory management practices comply with these regulations.

By following these steps, you can manage your inventory effectively and ensure that you have the right products on hand to meet demand while minimizing waste and avoiding overstocking.

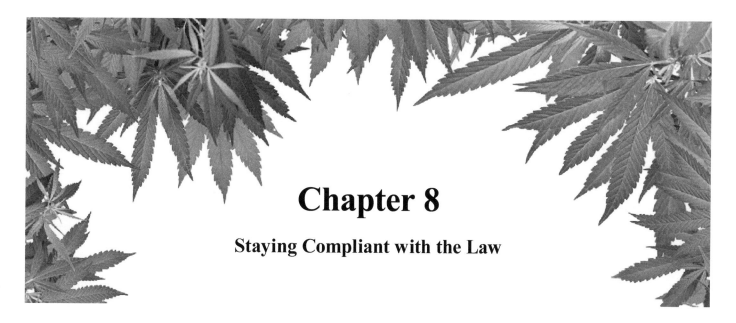

Chapter 8

Staying Compliant with the Law

The legal cannabis industry is highly regulated, and it is essential to stay compliant with the law. In this chapter, we will explore the different regulations that govern the cannabis industry. We will discuss how to stay compliant with the law and avoid legal issues.

Cannabis Business Regulations

The regulations that govern the cannabis business vary depending on the country, state, and even the municipality in which the business operates. Here are some of the regulations that commonly apply:

1. **Legalization:** The first and most important regulation is the legalization of cannabis for medical or recreational use. In some countries, cannabis is fully legal, while in others, it is only legal for medical use. In some countries, cannabis is still completely illegal.

2. **Licensing:** Cannabis businesses typically require licenses to operate legally. These licenses may be issued by the federal government, state government, or local municipality, depending on the jurisdiction.

3. **Product testing:** Cannabis products must be tested for potency, purity, and contaminants. Testing is typically done by thirdparty laboratories, and the results must be made available to regulators and consumers.

4. **Packaging and labeling:** Cannabis products must be packaged and labeled in accordance with regulatory standards. The packaging must be child-resistant and tamper-evident, and the label must include information about the product's potency, dosage, and potential side effects.

5. **Advertising and marketing:** Cannabis businesses are typically subject to strict advertising and marketing regulations. For example, they may be prohibited from advertising on certain platforms or using certain types of messaging.

6. **Security:** Cannabis businesses must take security measures to prevent theft and diversion of their products. This may include installing security cameras, hiring security personnel, and implementing inventory tracking systems.

7. **Taxation:** Cannabis businesses are typically subject to special taxes, such as excise taxes or sales taxes, that are specific to the cannabis industry.

It's important to note that regulations can vary widely depending on the jurisdiction and may be subject to change over time as laws evolve.

Compliance Tips for Cannabis

Staying compliant with the law in the cannabis business is essential to avoid legal and financial penalties, as well as to ensure the safety and well-being of customers and employees. Here are some tips on how to stay compliant:

1. **Know the laws and regulations:** The laws and regulations surrounding the cannabis industry can vary by state and country, so it's essential to research and understand the specific laws and regulations that apply to your business. This can include licensing requirements, packaging and labeling regulations, and security measures.

2. **Obtain necessary licenses and permits:** Ensure that your business has all the necessary licenses and permits required by the state or country in which you operate. This may include licenses for cultivation, distribution, and retail sales.

3. **Implement a robust compliance program:** Develop and implement a comprehensive compliance program that includes policies and procedures for maintaining compliance with all applicable laws and regulations. This can include measures to ensure product safety, employee training, record-keeping, and compliance audits.

4. **Conduct thorough background checks**: Conduct background checks on all employees and business partners to ensure that they do not have criminal records that would disqualify them from working in the industry.

5. **Ensure proper product testing and labeling:** Ensure that all cannabis products are tested for potency, contaminants, and other safety concerns. Also, ensure that all packaging and labeling comply with applicable regulations and provide accurate information about the product's contents and potency.

6. **Maintain adequate security measures:** Implement adequate security measures to prevent theft, diversion, and other unauthorized activities. This can include video surveillance, security alarms, and background checks for all employees.

7. **Stay up-to-date with changes in the law:** The laws and regulations surrounding the cannabis industry are constantly evolving, so it's essential to stay up-to-date with any changes and adjust your compliance program accordingly.

By following these tips and remaining vigilant about compliance, you can help ensure that your cannabis business operates legally and safely, while minimizing the risk of legal or financial penalties.

Conclusion

The legal cannabis industry presents numerous opportunities for entrepreneurs to make money. However, success in the cannabis business requires careful planning, a clear understanding of the legal framework, and effective management. This book provides a comprehensive guide to help you navigate the legal cannabis industry and build a successful business while staying within the bounds of the law.

Printed in the United States
by Baker & Taylor Publisher Services